THE
TWILIGHT
YEARS OF THE

GLASGOW

TRAM

A catalogue entry for this book is available from the British Library.
ISBN 1 874422 22 2

Published 1998 by
Adam Gordon,
Priory Cottage,
Chetwode,
Nr. Buckingham,
MK184LB

Printed by Drogher Press, Unit 4, Airfield Way, Christchurch, Dorset BH23 3TB

Typesetting by Trevor Preece, Gawcott, Buckingham.

LET GLASGOW FLOURISH

Trams have affected me strangely ever since I saw them running along the Victoria Embankment in my childhood. But one particular car journey I made with my sister through Glasgow in 1961 had a most unexpected result; for most of the way through the city we drove behind a modern green and orange coloured tram, which somehow inspired me into a determination to own one, and to see as much as I could of the tram system – by then sadly nearing the end of its twilight history. My explorations introduced me to the intimacies of the different tram styles, their rich and varied furnishings, their common bearing of the distinctive coat of arms with the words "Let Glasgow Flourish", the multifarious sounds from valves, brakes, compressors etc., the carved initials on the varnished woodwork (mild vandalism!), the destination blinds with unusual names like Normal School, and evocative names like Auchenshuggle, the individual smells, the rubber stair coverings and plastic handrails, the coloured glass, gilded lettering, bow collectors above and heavy bogies below….. Additionally it led me to know more about the city of Glasgow, and proved the old saying that it is the "friendliest city in the world"; I was particularly appreciative of the courtesy and kindness of Corporation staff on the trams, in the depots, and at the Head Office in Bath Street. It also resulted in my acquiring a streamlined double-deck Coronation tramcar no 1245 from Glasgow Corporation Transport.

I was an undergraduate at Oxford at the time, and money was somewhat tight. The complete tram cost £75 – quite a lot then. My parents were not keen to have the tram in their garden in Essex but after some months a fairy godfather in the form of Lord Montagu of Beaulieu agreed to transport and display the tram outside his new motor museum in Measham in the Midlands. For various reasons however it could not stay there long and after a few years it was transported to the East Anglia Transport Museum near Lowestoft.

Compressing history, over 30 years having elapsed since its acquisition, suffice it to say that the tram is now in need of considerable renovation and repair, and was moved earlier this year from Lowestoft to Blackpool. There is a possibility that it might run again there, but obviously a very large amount of money is required. One of the purposes of this book is to use part of the profits to fund the restoration.

My interest in trams eventually led to my starting up a business in second-hand transport material, and later on to publishing. Most of my professional life was spent specialising in criminal law, first at the Department of the Director of Public Prosecutions, and latterly at the Serious Fraud Office (from which I took early retirement), and I am hoping that in due course I shall be producing some transport books with a legal flavour. This Glasgow book however is the one I have most looked forward to publishing. It seemed apposite to coincide its publication with the centenary of the introduction of electric tramway traction on October 13th 1898. Nothing can ever replace the good old British tramcar in my affections, and Glasgow is surely much the poorer and less colourful and characterful without its "caurs". If I was dictator (!) I would certainly order a revival of the tram – though I find no beauty or aesthetic appeal in most of the modern vehicles produced today, which look to me as if they have been designed by mindless computers.

One of the advantages of my publishing and dealing business is the number of tramway enthusiasts and historians that I meet. One such is Alasdair Turnbull, a customer of many years' standing, who was the first person to offer his help in writing the captions for this book when I floated the idea through my quarterly booklist. I really am most grateful to him, and also to Ron Logan who has assisted in clarifying some topographical queries, also to Trevor Preece who has done some magical work during the scanning and pre-press processes. I have to apologise however for the quality of some of the pictures – the slides had not been looked after well before they came into my possession, and dust, mould and mishandling have caused some problems.

Apart from many other coloured slides from Douglas McMillan, I have also a large number of black and white negatives taken by him which could well source another book on the subject of the twilight years.

I do hope you enjoy this nostalgic backward look through these coloured pictures, together with the homely comments from Alasdair.

Finally, I would like to dedicate this book to all the people of Glasgow, and especially to those employed by the Corporation, as well as to all those others who remember the trams with affection and those who would love to see a true revival of the traditional double-deck tram – if Hong Kong can flourish with them today, why cannot Glasgow flourish again with them tomorrow?

Adam Gordon,
Priory Cottage, Chetwode,
Nr. Buckingham, Bucks, MK18 4LB
Tel: 01280 848650

September 1998

A CENTENARY CELEBRATION

It is earnestly hoped that this publication will come to press to coincide with the centenary of the inauguration of electric tramway traction in Glasgow on October 13th 1898. On that occasion, a procession of single deck "Room & Kitchen" or "But and Ben" single deck tramcars of American design, and two double deck prototype "Standard" trams ran from Mitchell Street to Springburn, with a party of dignitaries on board. The experiment was declared a success and it was formally decided by the Corporation to convert the whole undertaking from horse to electric traction. This was rushed through and completed by 1901 in time for the great International Exhibition of that year in the city.

The Room and Kitchen cars themselves caused problems, and by 1905 they had all been taken out of circulation, but the Standard trams were developed in stages to become the backbone of one of the most famous and successful tramway systems in the world.

With the exception of a brief successful appearance at the Garden Festival in 1988, trams have not run in the city since September 1962. Whilst the author feels this is regrettable, considering their environmental and economic advantages, electric traction still forms an important part of the transport infrastructure of Greater Glasgow in 1998, with the electric trains and electrified subway taking Glaswegians to and from work and other pursuits.

Members of the public can also look back in transport history at the magnificent Museum of Transport in the Kelvin Hall, Glasgow, where Room and Kitchen car 672 can be viewed in its Centenary year, along with horse car 543, Standard cars 779 and 1088, single deck experimental car 1089, Coronation car 1173, and Cunarder 1392, showing the development of the Glasgow tramcar over the years.

Car 672 was the original preservation project of the Scottish Tramway Museum Society (STMS), now the Scottish Tramway and Transport Society, formed in 1951. One of its members was W.Douglas McMillan, a keen photographer of tramways and railways. What better way to celebrate this centenary than to bring to light examples from this wonderful collection of colour slides mostly taken by Douglas in the "twilight years" of the tramway undertaking.

Car 672 in restored condition, in original livery, at the Glasgow Museum of Transport.

The very first electric tramcar in Glasgow – an early view of "Room & Kitchen" car 665, probably at the Mitchell Street terminus, with a policeman in attendance.

Car 672 became Mains Department Testing car 3. It is seen here in the brown livery of the Works cars, probably at Dalmarnock depot, where it spent much of its time latterly.

THE PHOTOGRAPHIC LEGEND OF DOUGLAS McMILLAN

Tramcars have fascinated me since I was a small boy. They passed beneath our top storey tenement window at 273, Paisley Road West, Glasgow, which looked towards Princes Dock, where world famous liners were repaired and refurbished.

As soon as my homework was done, however, I would station myself at the window, not to look at the ships but to observe and listen to the sights and sounds of the trams on services 21, 22, 32, 40 and at peak hours, service 12, as they went on their way to places such as Elderslie, Dumbreck, Maryhill, Bishopbriggs and Mount Florida.

My paternal grandfather, Alec Turnbull, was a proud Glaswegian who lived in the heyday of the trams. He instilled a love of these vehicles in me which has lasted a lifetime. I became a "tram enthusiast", joining the Scottish Tramway Museum Society in 1960, arming myself with notebook and camera on expeditions to tram termini and depots and on tours organised by the Society. I even persuaded my father to buy me some items from trams, but when I suggested a tram body for a greenhouse, he held up his hand...

I was aware, however, that this was very late on the scene, as by this time the Darnley right of way to Barrhead, the Airdrie/Coatbridge reservation, Cambuslang, Milngavie, even Paisley and Elderslie outposts of a once extensive system, had disappeared. So I listened avidly to the colourful recollections of older members of the Society, one of whom was W. Douglas McMillan.

Dougie, as he was known, was, like my grandfather, proud of his native city, especially of the railway tradition of Springburn, in which he lived, and of the tramcars. He was an early member of the Society, serving on its committee of which he was chairman several times, and he enriched the meetings and tours with his fund of stories and humorous anecdotes.

He took this one step further, however, for he was a skilled photographer. Often he would work the projector at meetings, using slides of his own and other members. Unknown to me at the time, he was building a vast personal photographic archive, which was used in publications up to his death in November 1994.

When in the Spring of 1997 Adam Gordon announced in his quarterly Collectors' catalogue that he had acquired a collection of slides taken by Dougie and asked for volunteers to identify them, I responded immediately, as I thought I would have a fair chance of success. So it was that 41 boxes containing 1563 slides, mostly in colour, arrived on my doorstep. It took me over seven months to go through them all, but eventually I did identify all but a handful of the scenes. As I did so, I was impressed by the quality of the slides and felt privileged to be given this task. This book is a presentation of 260 of these views, all in colour, except the archive photograph of Room and Kitchen car 665.

I hope readers will find the selection varied and interesting, and will not be disappointed if some locations are not included. All the main types of tram, and most of the places to which they ran, are covered. If readers have 10% of the pleasure I had looking through the slides, they are in for a treat. I hope, too, the book will appeal not just to tram enthusiasts but to members of the public who remember the trams themselves or, if too young to remember, have delighted in the recollections of those who were brought up with them.

Much of the character and personality of Douglas McMillan comes out in these views. Not for him boring "stills" of trams at termini, their crews standing rigidly to attention. We see the cars in crowded streets, on reserved track sections; we look down on them from railway and canal aqueduct bridges, such was the adventurous spirit of our photographer. He has caught many of his tramcar subjects clean, fresh from the paint shop, sparkling in the sunshine – yes the sun does shine in Glasgow! In January 1962 a small party of STMS members including Dougie and his lifelong friend Wilson Tennant, visited the original Edinburgh Transport Museum in East London Street. These two were a comedy duo, keeping the rest of the party in stitches with wisecracks and impersonations of the "Morningside accent". Something of this sense of humour comes out in the photos, especially one which is blurred but where he was not afraid to "have a go".

Readers who are not "tram buffs" may not be familiar with the terminology used to describe the trams, such as "Standard", "Hex dash", "Kilmarnock Bogie" etc. To you I would heartily recommend "The Glasgow Tramcar", by Ian G. McM. Stewart, which has become the Glasgow tram enthusiasts' "Bible", copies of which should be available from the Scottish Tramway and Transport Society, PO Box 78, Glasgow G3 6ER.

I have tried to present the views in an imaginative way, taking the form of a tour starting at Douglas

McMillan's home in Keppochill Road, Springburn, which is a happy coincidence as that is where the depot housing the original electric trams was located a century ago. We then go round the clock from 12 noon to 12 midnight, or round the points of the compass, taking in the locations as far as possible as you would have been able to do in the early to mid 1950's. To assist you, there follows on pages 10 and 11 a map issued by Glasgow Corporation Transport in 1951; because the original is too large to be conveniently reproduced in its full size, dimensions have been altered to suit the space.

If there are inaccuracies with any of the locations etc., I hope readers will excuse an exiled Glaswegian of some 32 years. I would certainly welcome comments on any aspect of the book – any reminiscences, memories etc., – indeed, some of the captions invite a response. Please write to me at the address given below.

This book has been compiled to celebrate the centenary of electric tramway traction in Glasgow; to provide funds for the restoration of car 1245; but, most of all, as a tribute to the photographic genius of W.Douglas McMillan.

Alasdair Turnbull,
5 Bennetts Walk,
Morpeth,
Northumberland, NE61 1TP

Acknowledgements
I wish to record grateful thanks to Ron Logan, of Carlisle, an exiled Glaswegian, for invaluable help in identifying some of the scenes and providing information; Sam Greer, of Morpeth, who once worked with the trams and my brother Ronnie, for loan of projectors; to Hector Soutter, of Ibrox, Glasgow, a former motorman, for memories; to the Morpeth Herald for the photograph of myself on the back cover; to my girlfriend Maureen Hughes, for her encouragement, and to Adam Gordon for giving me the opportunity to publish material on my lifelong interest.

Coronation car 1245 is seen in the twilight of its service years in Argyle Street, Finnieston, Glasgow.

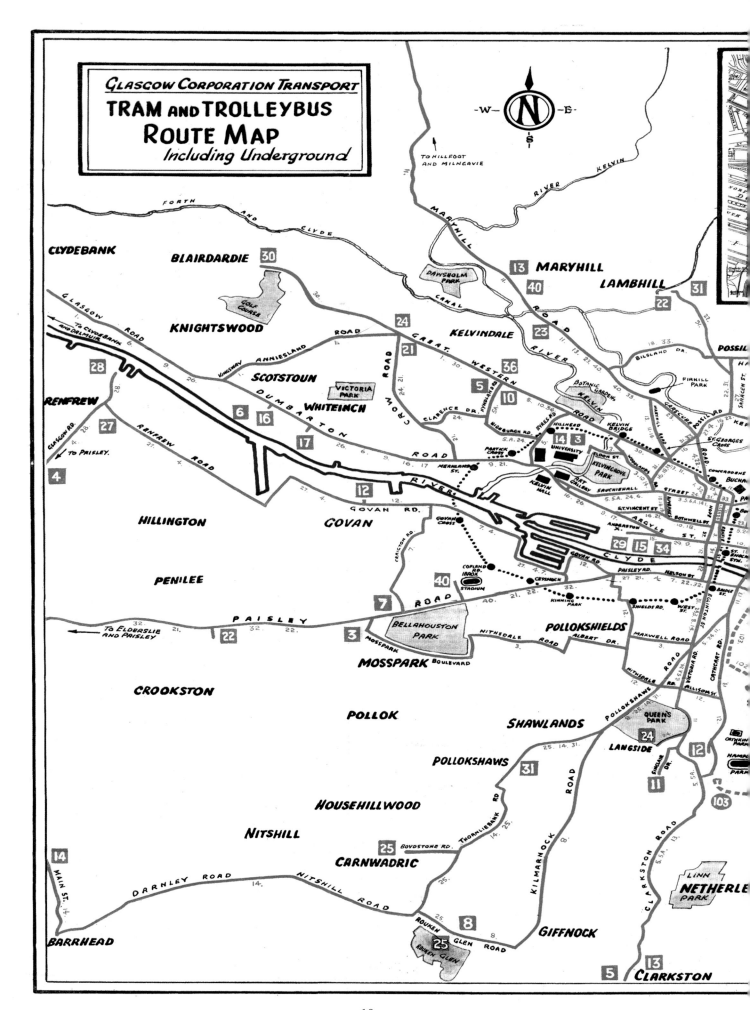

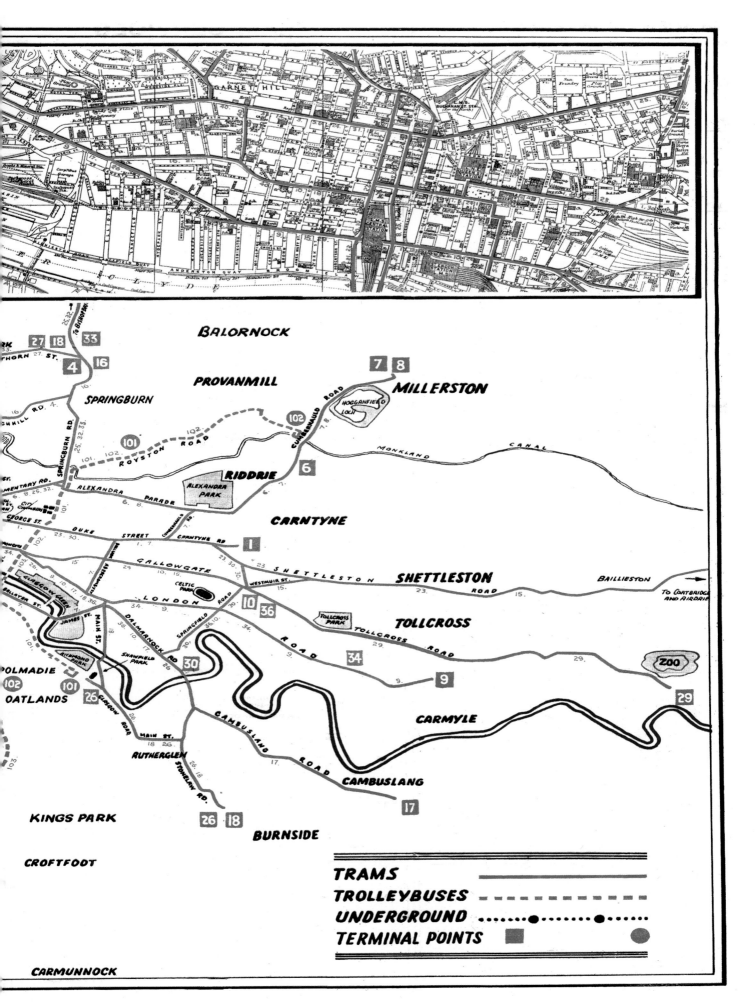

1.   Our journey starts outside W.D.McMillan's home in Keppochill Road, opposite Sighthill Cemetery, with the original Springburn depot in the background. Standard round dash car 376 is just leaving on a shortworking service 16 trip to Partick.

2.   Standard car 434 rounds the corner from Springburn Road into Keppochill Road on a sunny afternoon. Gas lamps still light the side street behind, in this evocative 1950's scene.

3.   Coronation Car 1236 speeds towards town on the open stretch of Springburn Road beyond the Hawthorn Street, Springburn terminus.

4.   Hex dash Standard car 1039 is seen a little further to the north with the tenements of Balgrayhill Road on the hillside.

5. A busy scene at the junction of Colston Road and Springburn Road with hex dash cars 9 and 108. The change in style of lamp standards in the distance tells us we are crossing from Glasgow into Lanarkshire. George Wimpey started building houses in Bishopbriggs in 1956 – my parents moved to the first detached villa in January 1957.

6. Standard car 223 is seen at the entrance to the Colston siding which was used for service cars only for a short time in 1954, and was the site of one of the Transport Department dumps.

7.	The screen has been changed for the return journey as 313 is about to follow a David Lawson Bristol Lodekka on the bridge over the Glasgow-Edinburgh railway at the entrance to Bishopbriggs; the Campsie Fells bask in the sunshine beyond.

8.	The same car on the same day passes Brackenbrae Road, its paintwork gleaming in the sunshine. I used this service on Sundays to travel from my new home in Bishopbriggs to Halfway for fiddle lessons with Mrs Jean White in Barlogan Avenue. One day I accidentally clouted a conductress with the fiddle case while climbing the stairs. She snapped "Watch whit ye're daein wi that thing, Yehudi!"

9.   Cunarder 1330 has just left Bishopbriggs terminus on the 25. Kirkintilloch Road is again deserted as in the last shot, except for the tram.

10.   Standard car 621 turns from Kirkintilloch Road into the Kenmure Avenue Bishopbriggs terminus. The bank on the corner was the site of a tram smash – does anyone remember when it occurred?

11.   We now head south for the next stage on our clockwise tour of Glasgow. Thirteen of their buses/coaches survive in various stages of preservation, mostly by members of "The MacBrayne Circle", with another four or five possibilities – including one in Australia! Standard car 217 is turning into Castle Street from Parliamentary Road with MacBraynes bus station behind.

12.   Coronation car 1171 heads east along Alexandra Parade passing the Wills cigarette factory. Note the lovely advertisement hoardings, many more of which we will see on our tour, the SMT AEC bus in the distance, and the street lighting on the span wires.

13. Another evocative fifties scene at the entrance gates to Alexandra Park with Coronation car 1167 on service 8 being overtaken on the (wrong!) offside by a Ford Zephyr saloon, with two other period pieces following.

14. A dark view in Cumbernauld Road, Riddrie, with Standard round dash car 388 on its return journey on the "yellow peril" service 7 from Millerston to Bellahouston. More of this later. The tracks here hugged the west side of the broad road.

15. Cunarder 1294, the second in the production line, passes Bennett & Fraser's sculptors yard in Cumbernauld Road at Riddrie Cemetery on service 8 on its way to Millerston.

16. A rural scene out past Riddrie at Hogganfield Loch, with Standard car 19 travelling cityward. The tracks here hug the east side of the road preventing other traffic overtaking on the left.

17.   Car 133 leans to the right as she mounts the hill approaching the junction with Robroyston Road – with an Alexander's bus disappearing over the brow of the hill.

18.   Hex dash car 161 has turned from the Millerston terminus into Cumbernauld Road. There was often a café at a tram terminus where you could stop off for a cuppa or scoff an ice cream before catching the car home.

19.   The Station Road Millerston terminus hosts two Cunarders and a Coronation car, with the wires of the replacement trolleybuses in place – service 7 is soon to go.

20.   Car 40 on service 40? – No, it's on a tour at Millerston. The revised single track stub layout made to accommodate the replacement service 106 trolleybuses can be clearly seen.

21.   Returning cityward ourselves, we pause at Paton Street to see Coronation car 1164 about to enter Dennistoun Depot. Note the unusual track layout to allow cars returning from the east to cross over, and those wonderful period advertisements again.

22.   This to me sums up Dougie McMillan's humorous outlook. Here he has crouched on a grassy embankment, at (I think?) Barrachnie, to catch a Coronation car at speed – not one for the purists, but I love it!

23.   Taken on a tour on experimental car 1005 on 4th March 1962 but it is Coronation car 1230 which steals the show as it almost comes out of the picture at you, leaving Baillieston terminus, its driver peering through the strong sunlight.

24.   Kilmarnock Bogie 1105 on a tour in 1955 uses the Baillieston terminus crossover on the private track to allow a Coronation car on service 15 to continue on its way from Airdrie to Anderston Cross.

25. 1105 at the Langloan crossover at the Coatbridge end of the reserved track over which exhilarating rides could be had, especially when an SMT bus was competing. This tour took 1105 along the Airdrie-Elderslie route on which the Kilmarnock Bogie cars were originally run.

26. This snowy scene is included here as it appears to be at Garrowhill, but readers out there, can you confirm please? It shows one of Glasgow's workhorse tramcars taking people home in the worst of weather conditions.

27.   Back in the City Centre for a moment, the motorman on car 1158 has his cab door open on a mild day in this Glasgow Cross scene, as he is about to pass the Tolbooth steeple at the junction of Trongate and High Street. Midland and Hackney (furniture) and Brighter Homes (home décor, etc) are two of the shops to which some of the people are heading.

28.   One of those scenes where you can "feel" the atmosphere as Coronation car 1279 passes the cinema in Gallowgate where musicals and comedy are top of the bill.

29.   Another atmospheric Gallowgate scene showing Coronation car 1200 crossing Bellgrove Street with a Central SMT Bristol Lodekka closing in on the near side. Some of the passengers on 1200 have spotted our photographer.

30.   I love this shot of the boy playing, oblivious of the Coronation car 1287 bearing down on him, returning to Parkhead Depot from a stint on service 29 on 14th October 1961.

31.   Coronation car 1279 was damaged substantially by fire twice in its life. It is seen here passing Tollcross Park on 27 October 1961.

32.   This and the following photograph were taken on the STMS car 500 tour on 5th March 1961. They convey the rural aspect of Tollcross terminus. Sadly, car 500 perished in the Dalmarnock Depot fire later that month.

33.   Coronation car 1238 clatters over the Tollcross crossover towards the photographer in brilliant sunshine.

34.   This shot of 1024 in Hamilton Road, between Tollcross and Broomhouse, is the only one of an ex-Liverpool Green Goddess car in the collection of over 1,500 slides. Whether Dougie did not particularly like them, or reserved them more for prints, I do not know.

35.   Standard car 283 shows service no "15" as she leaves Broomhouse, passing the entrance to Calderpark Zoo. Cars on this section carried a warning "To monkeys and other primates" that "swinging from strap to strap inside the car is strictly forbidden"!? (Apologies for the orange livery having turned pink – owing to bleaching of the transparency.)

36.   245 on a tour has been taken as far as the motorman dared at Broomhouse terminus. Note the uncollected fares box on the platform. This area has changed beyond recognition following the construction of the motorway intersection.

37.   We retrace our steps to look at another tour photograph, this time of rebuilt Kilmarnock Bogie car 1100 in Abercrombie Street, alongside a GCT Leyland bus. By this time, service 7 has succumbed to the trolleybuses.

38.   This was a favourite spot of Dougie's; there were at least five pictures to choose from. It is at Bridgeton Cross, in sunshine again. 118 is on a shortworking trip to Scotstoun but the conductor has not changed the lower screen.

39.   The taxi in the previous scene has gone and Standard round dash car 988 has appeared going the whole way on what became Glasgow's last tram service.

40.   Coronation car 1285 approaches Bridgeton Cross on London Road, showing some signs of wear & tear as typified the trams in their "Twilight Years". Despite this, they gave sterling service, and Glaswegians still fondly remember them as the new millennium approaches.

41. Taken on an STMS tour on 29th April 1962 to record the sounds of the trams, single deck bogie car 1089, known as "Bailie Burtts" car, takes a breather at that most famous location, Auchenshuggle terminus. The car survives as a static exhibit in Glasgow's Museum of Transport in the Kelvin Hall.

42. Another survivor, this time at the French tramways museum in the outskirts of Paris, Standard car 488 is caught in the sunshine outside Dalmarnock Depot.

43.　A splendid close-up of Cunarder car 1313 leaving Dalmarnock Depot to enter service. 1313 was the last car to run in service from Yoker to this depot on September 1st 1962.

44.　An atmospheric shot by Dougie of a Coronation car crossing Dalmarnock Bridge heading for Burnside, with the skeleton-like construction of Dalmarnock Power Station in the background.

45.   Into Rutherglen burgh now where a lady passenger grasps the platform pole for a helping hand as she boards Coronation car 1285. We have left the grim, grey tenements of Dalmarnock behind, and now pass superior ones of sandstone construction.

46.   The trim lines of Cunarder car 1307 are highlighted in this view at Menzies Street fare station on 21st May 1961. Services 18 and the portion of service 26 from Farme Cross to Burnside were withdrawn two weeks later.

47.   Another STMS tour shot taken at Farme Cross, on 28 May 1961, where the number blinds on 1115 have been turned to 17, though the service had ceased on 18th November 1958.

48.   It's a warm day and the driver of Coronation car 1158 has the cab door open (again!) as he heads away from Rutherglen Cross along Stonelaw Road on the final stage of his journey to Burnside. Scooters have recently become popular in this country again.

49.   No date given on this excellent close-up of Standard car 12 at Burnside, again in brilliant sunshine. Are you there?

50.   I've included this view of 1115 on tour at Burnside as the intrepid photographer standing behind the tram is myself. I still have the Brownie "Cresta" camera and the calf coloured holdall, though not used now.

51.   A short diversion on the Shawfield section of service 18 now, and we see the highest numbered car in the fleet, Coronation car 1398 with ex-Liverpool trucks, on Rutherglen Bridge.

52.   Back at Bridgeton Cross and Cunarder 1315 is in rather shabby condition as she leads BUT Trolleybus TR93... The long defunct Evening Citizen was running a strip feature on the famous England footballer Stanley Matthews.

53.   We are now making for the South side of Glasgow and see Standard car 302 in James Street Bridgeton on the "7".

54.   Out on Glasgow Green, 156 has the road to herself as she travels west along King's Drive on a special service to Bellahouston.

55.   On King's Bridge, 266 glints in the sunlight, Bellahouston-bound. Service 7, nicknamed "the yellow peril", served the toughest districts in Glasgow – Govan, the Gorbals, Calton and Barlinnie Prison in Riddrie – you probably all know that!

56.   We have returned to the city centre for a moment and see round dash car 288 in Jamaica Street, probably like many of these views, on a Sunday. Grant's Furniture Store is beyond the tram.

57.   We are heading south now and Standard car 88 passes Paisley's Department Store, alas no more, even the building has been demolished.

58.   199 looking very smart and fully laden, is crossing Jamaica or Glasgow Bridge towards Paisley's. The shop blinds are down now, so it is probably a Sunday. The Smedleys Peas advert was one of my favourites.

59.   Standard car 658 gleams in the sun as she heads north up Eglinton Street on the 24 to Anniesland, again, filled with passengers. The buildings here have now almost completely disappeared.

60.   You can almost hear the squeal as 235 rounds the tight curve from Turriff Street into Eglinton Street on the 5. The advert for the mass X-Ray campaign has a personal touch – my father was a radiologist at Stobhill and the Southern General Hospitals at this time.

61.   One of the last batch of Coronations – 1393 – is turning from Turriff Street into Pollokshaws Road at the St Andrew's Print Works. Gray Dunn made the "Blue Riband" biscuit – a favourite all over Britain.

62.   1395 is seen just round the corner alongside the St. Andrew's Printworks, 197 Pollokshaws Road, where Glasgow Corporation Printing Department produced the tram timetables, amongst other things.

63.   Cunarder 1305 leaves Eglinton Toll in Victoria Road on the 24 to Langside. The Ovaltine advert tones in nicely with the colour scheme on the car. It was dinner jackets only at the Plaza Ballroom.

64.   Standard car 32 heads along the short paved stretch of reserved track in Battlefield Road in this fascinating view of an historic area. In the distance is the Corporation tram shelter which features in picture postcards and still survives.

65.   A hex dash Standard car rounds the long bend in Cathcart Road, having left the Mount Florida terminus of service 12.

66.   A lovely shot of Coronation car 1265 taken on a tour on 12th August 1956, turning from Cathcart Road into the single track section on Prospecthill Road used by football specials for Hampden Park and to gain access to Langside Depot.

67.   A brisk walk takes us to Shawlands Cross to cover the routes serving some of Glasgow's more affluent suburbs. 124 is in clear focus but the Coronation car, with its original louvre over the driver's window, is a little blurred as she clatters over the points.

68.   We stop off at Newlands Depot now to view a transparency taken by the late M.H. Waller of the Leeds Transport Historical Society of Experimental Car no 1005 "The Blue Devil" in its original front entrance rear exit form and livery. Contrast this with view no 92 at Albert Drive showing the car in its final form.

69.   Another beauty from the Leeds Group at Newlands – Experimental Lightweight car no 1001 gleams in the sunshine taken in 1949 by the late M.H.Waller. These cars were later transferred to Elderslie.

70.   Douglas McMillan's view of preserved horse car 543 in Newlands Depot yard. It ran in the final procession of cars on 4th September 1962 and is now in the Museum of Transport at the Kelvin Hall, Glasgow.

71.   Six mostly youthful (!) tramway enthusiasts sit on the top deck of 543. I think I recognise David L. Thomson third from the left, but would be delighted if anyone can name the others.

72.   We are back on the road again, at Merrylee terminus in Kilmarnock Road with car 502, its paintwork gleaming and a Western Leyland bus approaching. Note the span wire street lighting as in Alexandra Parade etc.

73.   Hex dash car 152 at the same location. "AAAAH BISTO!" was another of my favourite adverts – it's still with us!

74.   A quick run through Giffnock and we are at Rouken Glen terminus, where Cunarder 1322 is waiting to take us on the 25 to Thornliebank, Pollokshaws and beyond. This was a popular Sunday day out destination for Glaswegians in the tramway era.

75.   The Cunarder car in this leafy scene is 1293, the first one produced, proceeeding along Spiersbridge Road.

76.   The motorman on Standard car 62 takes a look down Boydstone Road before crossing from Main Street Thornliebank into Thornliebank Road. The camber in the road is well illustrated here.

77.   262 is at the same junction but about to set off down Boydstone Road for Carnwadric terminus. I always thought "Carnwadric" sounded more like an Anglo-Saxon warrior's name than a Glasgow place name.

78.   Car 217 at Carnwadric terminus outside the shops in Boydstone Road. This was one of the last extensions in Glasgow, opened on November 7th 1948, originally for new service 14B.

79. A clear shot of Coronation car 1241 having crossed the railway bridge above Thornliebank station, with the new Hillpark housing development behind.

80. A little further on towards Pollokshaws, 1954 built Coronation car 1394 is seen in Thornliebank Road with the spire of Eastwood Church in Mansewood peeping above the trees.

81.   An unidentified Coronation car slowly makes its way along Harriett Street, Pollokshaws, which has an olde-worlde atmosphere about it.

82.   A busy scene at Cross Street, Pollokshaws, with Cunarder 1336 and Coronation 1256 heading for Rouken Glen and Arden respectively, while 1241 is on a short working to Castle Street.

83.   A hex-dash car, possibly 231, waits in the little used "Pollokshaws" stub in Nether Auldhouse Road. The granite setts and point-work are clean as this was opened towards the end of 1952.

84.   Cunarder 1333 passes Pollokshaws Road Post Office near Greenview Street on May 10th 1959; service 25 was withdrawn four weeks later. Greenview Street provided access to Newlands Depot.

85.   Standard car 35 approaches "The Old Swan Inn" in Pollokshaws Road at Haggs Road, passing a magnificent row of advertisement hoardings. Whatever happened to "Jean MacGregor"?

86.   Coronation 1171 in Pollokshaws Road being overtaken by a very smart Austin A55 car.

87.   Shawlands Cross is in the distance as hex-dash car 217 passes school buildings on 10th May 1959.

88.   The overhead of the single track section in Coplaw Street is just visible to the right as is Larkfield bus garage in the distance in this view of car 128 in Pollokshaws Road.

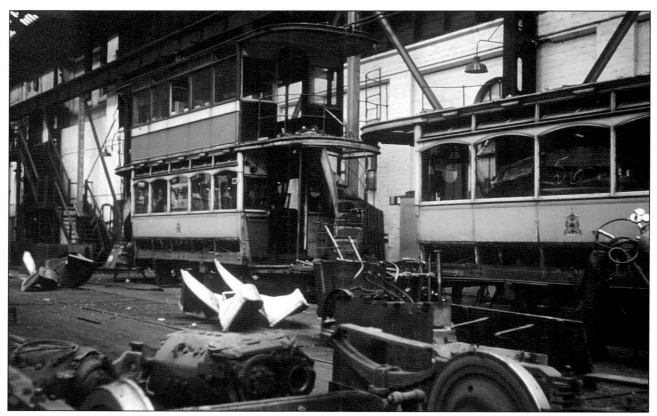

89.   We are now at Coplawhill Works and take a breather to look round there. Unfortunately, it's not a pleasant sight as two Standard cars have completed their "twilight years" and are being scrapped.

90.   This Coronation tram, 1215 or 1275, looks to have been in an accident as it is viewed by young Hamish Cormack, resplendent in kilt, the son of the long time Scottish Tramway Museum Society secretary Ian Cormack and his wife Margaret. Sadly, Hamish died in a tragic accident but he is still fondly remembered by his family and tramway enthusiasts.

91.   All the trams in this scene are still alive, for these are preserved in the Glasgow Museum of Transport, and the National Tramway Museum at Crich, Derbyshire. They are seen here in the paint shop at Coplawhill.

92.   Outside in Albert Drive, Experimental car 1005 is seen in its final condition (see view no.68).

93.   Car 1089 is posed on the bridge over the railway with, if my memory serves me correctly, Inspector William Wilson on the left. He acted as motorman on many of the enthusiast tram tours.

94.   Brrrr!! An icy scene outside Coplawhill Works with ex-Paisley School car 1017. Meetings of the Scottish Tramway Museum Society were held in this car for a while. It is now being substantially restored at the Summerlee Industrial Heritage Museum, Coatbridge.

95.   Works car No.37, a sett wagon used by the Permanent Way Department to carry "setts" or cobblestones to places where track was being renewed, is seen in Albert Drive outside Coplawhill Works. In the background – the timber yard, offices, works canteen and the entrance to the Permanent Way yard in Barrland Street.

96.   We are back with the service cars now and see Cunarder 1333 in Maxwell Road bound for Mosspark, dwarfed by the huge gasometer.

97.   Dougie's shutter has come down just as Cunarder 1308 passes the twin lamps outside the Lord Provost's residence in Nithsdale Road, Pollokshields, with a lovely ?Morgan sports car in the foreground.

98.   Coronation car 1222 passes Sherbrooke Avenue with the Sherbrooke Hotel to the right. My school pal Richard Sykes, another staunch young supporter of the tramway cause, lived near here.

99. Generally, more modern cars were used on service 3 in the "twilight years" as it passed through the affluent Pollokshields suburb, but Standard cars appeared now and then and 363 is seen heading along the Mosspark Boulevard reservation with the Mosspark housing scheme behind.

100. Another view of the reserved track looking east, with Standard car 100 alongside Bellahouston Park. Even the older trams seemed to glide along here.

101. Standard car 520 is caught in the sunlight back in Albert Drive, about to turn sharply into Kenmure Street; the single track leading to Coplawhill can be seen to the right.

102. Lots of interest here in this Shields Road scene, as flush panelled car 27 on service 12 descends slowly past the ornate centre poles toward Scotland Street. In the background is a striking (!) church clock tower and in the distance, the huge shipyard crane at Finnieston, still there today, but silent.

103. Another of Dougie's well-painted tram subjects, no 702, is seen from the top deck of a service 12 car in Milnpark Street, near the former Kinning Park Depot, from which the sand works cars operated.

104. We have turned into Paisley Road West and are in "home" territory, for I lived at no.273 until I was ten years old. Nicely painted (again!) 780 has just passed Bellahouston Academy, which was my school in these years.

105. A little further to the west, 306 is passing a Boys Brigade parade on the march, probably from Ibrox Church in Clifford Street to Bellahouston Park. The Ford Prefect car behind the bus is identical to my father's first family car, bought in 1950 – I was envied by my school pals then!

106. Further out alongside Bellahouston Park, the venue of the Empire Exhibition of 1938, car 359 crosses the junction with Jura Street, created for use by services serving the Exhibition.

107. 269 heading citywards at Halfway. One of the block of flats known as the Moss Heights can just be seen to the left – these were the first post-war high-rise flats in Glasgow.

108. Out past Crookston, terminus of the 22 and latterly 32, services, car 381 heads along Glasgow Road, Ralston, for Elderslie. The trim bungalows and villas were selling new for £525 upwards in 1932 and were advertised as having "a lovely situation – excellent bus and tram service – adjacent to Ralston golf course."

109. Same area with Cunarder 1386, perhaps about to race the Western bus alongside. Former motorman Hector Soutter remembers the astonished expression on the face of a Western bus driver ("his jaw dropped!") as he overtook him in his Coronation tram doing c.50mph one day near here.

110. Coronation car 1273 passes the perimeter of Barshaw Park, Ralston. I completed my only full round of golf here with two school friends, taking 133 strokes – out in 68, back in 65!!

111. Cunarder 1354 is seen a little to the west near the entrance gates to Barshaw Park – as in the last scene, there is no other traffic about.

112. Taken from the top of a tram heading for the City Centre St. Vincent Street terminus of service 21, Cunarder 1357 has passed the Park and is approaching Hawkhead Road, which at one time was the terminus of the Paisley and District tramways.

113. There are a few passengers walking out to board as Standard car 986 pulls up opposite the shops in Glasgow Road in the Williamsburgh district of Paisley. Paisley Ice Rink, where I had my one and only skating experience, is situated nearby.

114. One of the Elderslie Depot batch of Coronations, 1271, shows its "nose up, tail down" as it clatters over the east-west tracks at Paisley Cross, on service 28 en route for Glenfield.

115. The road sign on the left shows we are near Paisley Infirmary as Coronation car 1278 drones past the shops in Neilston Road, Paisley. A McGills bus is in the distance.

116. Not far from Glenfield terminus now, the chimney stacks of industrial Paisley can be seen as Coronation car 1283 slows to let off a passenger.

117. It's a rural scene as Standard car 398 is about to climb the hill to Glenfield.

118. Glenfield terminus looking towards Paisley, with Coronation car 1286 waiting to leave for Renfrew Ferry. This was a popular place especially on a Sunday to begin a walk to the Gleniffer Braes.

119. In the shopping centre with mainly shoe shops in evidence, Standard car 463 passes the lay-bye in High Street, Paisley. Here again the street lighting is suspended from the tram span wires.

120. Coronation car 1271 seen in the company of Morris, Austin and Hillman motor cars passing small shops opposite the Coats Thomas Memorial Church, where High Street leads into Wellmeadow Street, Paisley.

121. A busy traffic scene at the entrance to Woodlands Cemetery, Ferguslie, as Cunarder 1357 passes Coronation 1271 in Broomlands Street.

122. Elderslie terminus, with Standard 381 alongside Coronation car 1271 (again!) taken by Dougie from another tram waiting to cross over. The 21 was a fairly frequent service, originally terminating at Anniesland.

123. A visit to Elderslie Depot showing ex-Paisley car 1068 with screens showing two destinations it would have served in its earlier days of Glasgow Corporation ownership. The car, now in original restored condition as Paisley no.68, is a regular performer at the National Tramway Museum, Crich, Derbyshire (see view no. 256).

124. Experimental "Lightweight" car no.6, the last one of five built as a cheaper alternative to the Coronation cars, in Elderslie Depot yard. They were not judged to be a success and were used only sparingly here, on rush hour and special runs.

125. "The tram that went to America", Coronation 1274, is seen in Renfrew Road on the northern outskirts of Paisley, near St. Margaret's Convent. It is now at the Seashore Trolley Museum, Connecticut, USA.

126. Standard car 146 at Paisley North or "Sandyford", with open country beyond. The car is quite well filled, as befits service 28 which was nicknamed "the goldmine" as it was well used by locals, even in the face of competing buses. Paisley "Buddies" loved the trams too, and thousands turned out after midnight on 12 May 1957 to say goodbye as the last car, no.1277, made its way from Renfrew Ferry to Elderslie depot.

127. Standard car 108 has just left Paisley North on the 4 and is about to pass Coronation 1272 on the "Goldmine". The Coronations could show their paces on the wide, open stretches of road here, causing conductresses to question their drivers' sanity at times!

128. 108 nears Paisley North on this stretch. This car was another casualty of the Dalmarnock Depot fire in 1961. When I was 9, my father took me to look at new housing here but I spent most of the time admiring the passing trams!

129. Standard car 455 and Coronation 1282 in Renfrew Road just south of Porterfield Road. Looks like the bowler hatted gent and the lady are waiting for a 28 into Paisley.

130. Standard car 57 waits to take on passengers at the junction of Porterfield Road and Renfrew Road while two ladies with a pram have already started to cross in front. "Mr. Therm" boasts the advantages of Gas Hot Water in the advert on the side of the tram. Among the interesting row of buildings is a Post Office doubling as an Ironmonger and tobacconist, and behind them lies a cinema.

131. Kilmarnock Bogie 1105 sits at the far end of the Porterfield Road siding built to allow trams to convey the hundreds of workers home from the nearby Babcock and Wilcox works. Service 34 had three changes during its short life from 1946 to 1952 but it was mostly in the East End.

132. Car 265 passes a variety of housing in Hairst Street Renfrew on its way south. How shopping habits have changed with the coming of supermarkets!

133. Flush panelled Standard car 143 swings round into High Street, Renfrew, in front of the imposing edifice of Renfrew Town Hall, with its arched windows and balcony. Behind, a Cunningham's AEC bus passes the unusually styled outfitter's building.

134. 909 appears to be leaving Renfrew Ferry terminus as the conductress adjusts the screen – looks like she's been kept busy!

135. A very smart Standard car 260 seen at approximately the same spot from the other side of Ferry Road. It is probably returning to Elderslie Depot which always took pride in the appearance of its cars and had a homespun family atmosphere about it.

136. 1270 and another Coronation car from the Elderslie allocation lie over at the Ferry, with the distinctive huge electricity pylon towering above Coia's café.

137. We have come along the long open stretch exposed to high winds past Renfrew Aerodrome and Hillington Road and see car 341, which has just rounded the corner between two road islands in Renfrew Road, Shieldhall.

138. Standard car 643 waits in the single track Shieldhall terminus in Bogmoor Road under the shadow of the SCWS buildings. There is something slightly eerie about this scene – it would be different at tea time when all the workers would crowd onto the trams lined up here.

139. Car 101 advertises the timeless Dulux paints as it heads cityward along Renfrew Road, Shieldhall. The single track leading off to the right with no overhead was used by a steam locomotive carrying materials for Stephens' shipyard.

140. Looking back towards Shieldhall, car 102 is fully laden as she is about to pass the Southern General Hospital.

141. A scene at Linthouse with lots of interest, as car 32 passes some colourful advertisements while a Vauxhall saloon eases past two cyclists; with an old man tapping his unhurried way along the pavement.

142. We take a diversion down Craigton Road now on the final section of the "7" and see 121 passing a row of prefabs after a heavy shower on 16th February 1958. Prefabs were erected in large numbers just after the war and were basic but popular.

143. A few yards down the road, and the sun has come out in full again as a Standard hex dash car with a number in the 40's leans over to turn into Jura Street.

144. Standard car 67 in Jura Street at Bunessan Street – one of many street names here with Argyll connections. This stretch of track from Craigton Road was added to provide services to and from the great Empire Exhibition in Bellahouston Park in 1938.

145. A lady walks unhurriedly towards Standard tramcars (67 and 183) at Bellahouston terminus. The "7" was a busy service and photographs often show two or three cars bunched together.

146. This is a dark photograph but I've included it as it is in the heart of Govan and shows the entrance to the goods yard used by the Fairfield electric locomotive (illustrated in the next scene) to transport materials to and from their yard. Govan is now more famous for its philosophical resident, Rab. C. Nesbitt.

147. The Fairfield electric locomotive is seen on an enthusiasts' tour in 1962 outside the goods yard, after the withdrawal of trams from Govan in November 1958. There is bunting about so it could have been during the Govan Fair, part of which was a street procession I remember vividly as a child.

148. Yet another smartly painted tram is caught by Dougie's camera as it rounds the sharp bend in Govan Road at Summertown Road alongside Princes Dock. The tenements in the background have been demolished to make way for lower density housing.

149. A good view of the shipping in the dry dock could be had from the top deck of a tram – as illustrated in this photo of Standard car 183 on Govan Road. The tenements of Plantation can be seen in the distance – most of these have disappeared too.

150. An excellent close-up of car 126, fully laden on the "7", passing an AEC Regent Corporation bus, again alongside Princes' Dock. This area came to life again briefly with tramcars during the Glasgow Garden Festival in 1988.

151. Standard car 238 rounds the corner at Lorne School, with the track used by rush hour cars on service 12 in the foreground, and Govan Depot in nearby Brand Street. This was part of the view from my top storey tenement living room window in Paisley Road West.

152. Heading back into town, we have a splendid view of Cunarder 1341 crossing the King George V Bridge, opened on 27th February 1928 to relieve congestion from Jamaica Bridge.

153. We linger awhile amongst the shops in Argyle Street to see car 488, which has just passed Lewis's, Scotland's biggest Department store at the time. Jackson the tailor, alas no more, provided quality suits which Ron Logan, who helped me immensely with this publication, wore with pride.

154. Crowds fill Argyle Street now in this view from the steps of St. Enoch Station. Trains for Fort William left from Queen Street Station but were advertised here. Do you fancy some lunch in "His Lordship's Larder"?

155. Bellies full, we step out into Argyle Street again to see a row of Coronation cars headed by 1221 and 1257 crossing the Union Street/Jamaica Street junction, the busiest in Glasgow at one time. "The thinking man reads the Glasgow Herald" according to the advertisement.

156. A shaft of pink sunlight adds colour to this view at the same junction looking up Union Street, with smartly painted car 120 heading for Kelvinside. I remember seeing Stanley Baxter in pantomime at the Alhambra Theatre in 1955, as a tram conductress mimicking the "Pan loaf accent" of the residents of that suburb.

157. Car 3, with no destination or number screens, is about to pass under "the Heilanman's Umbrella". It looks too clean to be going to Coplawhill Works for scrap, so perhaps it is doing a depot change here.

158. Coronation car 1279 carrying a full load, comes from the "Umbrella" out into the sunlight to turn into Hope Street, followed by a lovely flat-fronted coach with a Dundee registration.

159. Taken on the last day of tram services to Farme Cross, 22nd October 1961, 1174 pulls out from under the "Umbrella". This was the last car to leave Auchenshuggle terminus on the evening of 4th September 1962, prior to the final procession of trams from Dalmarnock Depot to Coplawhill Works.

160. An excellent W.D.McMillan close-up of Standard car 50 on a "special", rounding the corner from Hope Street into Argyle Street.

161. We pause here for another view, of Standard car 625 on service 10. A blurred Kilmarnock bogie car is disappearing to the right. The double lamp standard was more typical of the style used in e.g. Shettleston Road or Great Western Road.

162. A view entirely changed today, of Anderston Cross terminus in Stobcross Street with car 488 waiting to cross over. The busy Clydeside Expressway now occupies this site, but Cheapside Street reminds us of the disastrous whisky bond fire in March 1960 which claimed 19 lives.

163. We proceed up Hope Street now and see a trench coated gent sprint across in front of Standard car 141, with a "Green Goddess" tram in the distance.

164. A reminder of one purpose of this book, i.e. to provide funding towards the restoration of Coronation car 1245, seen here in afternoon sunshine outside the "Daily Record" offices in Hope Street. Vernon Street was a destination not often seen on the screens.

165. The sun shines brightly on Coronation 1284 as she crosses from Elmbank Street into Bothwell Street, at the junction with St. Vincent Street. Behind lie the buildings of Glasgow High School for Boys, which I attended from 1959 to 1964.

166. Another view of the same location showing Cunarder 1312 on service 16. We could hop on and ride back to Douglas's home in Springburn, but there is still much to see.

167. Past the High School and the King's Theatre, we have turned into Sauchiehall Street and see Coronation car 1216 just west of Charing Cross, on the "6" to Alexandra Park.

168. A splendid photograph at the same location showing Standard car 366 going west. Behind can be seen the buildings of the Grand Hotel, tragically swept away to make way for the M8 motorway, and Charing Cross Mansions which were spared.

169. Looking west along Sauchiehall Street, car 812 which is still going strong at the National Tramway Museum, approaches. Many of the terraced buildings here were used by doctors and dentists as surgeries.

170. A slight diversion to the loop at Finnieston to see Coronation car 1269 on an STMS tour, with myself as a junior member third from the right on the top deck, and David L. Thomson, author of "A handbook of Glasgow Tramways" surveying the car, from the street, his arms akimbo.

171.   A parade including women and children stops the traffic including a Cunarder tram in Argyle Street at Hastie Street. They could be heading for the Kelvin Hall nearby.

172.   Another close-up past the Kelvin Hall with the University tower peeping from behind the Western Infirmary, showing car 1222 on a short working on service 9.

173. This view, taken from the railway bridge carrying the Glasgow Low Level "Blue Trains", to me conveys the atmosphere of the thriving shopping centre in Partick, with trams in the distance.

174. There is a strong Scottish influence in the vehicles pictured here in Dumbarton Road, Partick, as Hurst Nelson built Kilmarnock bogie trams 1091 and 1103 pass each other with an Albion lorry and Albion CX19 Corporation bus behind.

175. Dumbarton Road is wider here at Whiteinch, where we see Kilmarnock Bogie 1117 rumbling along on its way to Auchenshuggle.

176. The Whiteinch terminal stub in Primrose Street, with Coronation car 1269 and a rather pre-occupied boy. The Scotstoun Emporium was the scene of another tram smash involving a Kilmarnock Bogie car.

177. This scene, a little further along Dumbarton Road towards Scotstoun, is included to show some work being done in the cobbled road, with traffic still passing. Track maintenance was usually carried out at night, with works cars in attendance.

178. The prototype Kilmarnock Bogie car 1090 is seen near Scotstoun tram terminus. She was one of the last survivors of her class, their large carrying capacity being ideal for transporting queues of shipyard workers home.

179. Out in Yoker, Kilmarnock Bogie 1105 is in service now and not looking so smart as in the 1955 tour views.

180. The last ten Kilmarnock Bogies were built by Brush of Loughborough and 1138 is seen here in Dumbarton Road, Yoker, with few passengers on board.

181. The last "last car". This is September 6th 1962, and Clydebank Corporation are staging their own farewell to the trams which served their burgh so well. Coronation 1282, a survivor at Crich, was chosen for this occasion and was driven by Motorman William Trotter, from the Town Hall where it is seen here, to the burgh boundaries and back with dignitaries on board, before returning to Coplawhill Works with the General Manager's son as the only passenger.

182. Looks like 1151 is the Coronation car stopping to allow a passenger to step off on the approach to Dalmuir.

183. An excellent view of Standard car 447 as she crosses the swing bridge over the Forth and Clyde Canal at Dalmuir on a service 1 peak time journey.

184. Hurst Nelson Kilmarnock Bogie car 1108 has just left Dalmuir West terminus and is passing the Mount Blow Bar at the start of its 12 mile journey to Auchenshuggle. There are still gaps in the housing in this area, which suffered extensively in the Clydebank Blitz of March 1941.

185. A battered Cunarder 1365 waits to leave Dalmuir West terminus. Two adverts on the car extol the virtues of electricity in the home.

186. The "Room and Kitchen" motif of the Scottish Tramway Museum Society is proudly displayed on Coronation car 1269 on its tour of the little that was left of a once extensive tramway system at Dalmuir West, on 27th May 1962.

187. 1051 was a late Standard hex dash survivor, its life no doubt extended a little further by the Dalmarnock Depot fire in March 1961. It is seen here in the broad expanse of Kingsway, not far from the Scotstoun West terminus of service 1, which occasionally ran to Dalmarnock.

188. There were no slides of the reserved track on Great Western Road in Dougie's collection, but the broad vista of Great Western Road is well portrayed in this shot of Standard car 186, with another Standard and a Coronation car in the distance. The Coronation will be turning into Kelvinside terminus, as none were used on the "1" and "30" because of tight bends in the East End.

189. Standard car 662 is smartly painted as she picks up speed after crossing Cleveden Road on Service 1.

190. Car 121 seen nearer the city in Great Western Road, at Kirklee.

191. Service 30 is represented here by this wonderful shot of 274 and 17 passing each other at the brow of the hill on Great Western Road beyond Byres Road.

192. The number on this Coronation car is indistinct but it has just crossed the Byres Road junction with Great Western Road on service 10.

193.   The tramlines still lead off into Byres Road for use by Service 5 cars in this excellent view of car 187 passing the ornate building at the entrance to the Botanic Gardens. Steam rises from a train using the station below.

194.   Standard car 252 has turned from Woodlands Road into Park Road passing sandstone tenements typical of Glasgow's West End. This became the terminus of service 3 after closure of the railway bridge in Eldon Street.

195. 287 leans into the bend at the same spot, heading in the opposite direction. Near here, in Glasgow Street, Kelvinbridge, lived a school pal of mine named Ronald Edgar. Together we formed a "Tramway Club" and enjoyed a tour of most of the remaining system early in 1960.

196. Back in the city centre now, Standard car 384 turns from Sauchiehall Street into Cambridge Street, passing Reid and Todd, one of the many famous names of Department Stores in this excellent shopping centre.

197. A superb shot of Standard car 165 rounding the corner from Sauchiehall Street into Renfield Street. Lauder's Bar was patronized by stars and staff of the Pavilion, Empire and Lyric Theatres all within sight of it. It still serves excellent meals and features Sir Harry Lauder, perhaps the most famous Scottish entertainer of all, in its wall displays.

198. The classic view, this time in colour, of the Glasgow Corporation Transport Headquarters at 46 Bath Street, with Standard car 44 travelling down Renfield Street. Full details of the tram and bus services were displayed on the windows.

199. A view which to my mind captures wonderfully Glasgow's tramcars at the heart of its city life, right among the people. They are so much a part of the way of life that her citizens are unconcerned that a tramcar is bearing down on them. 271 turns from Renfield Street into St. Vincent Street.

200. The conductor is signalling a right hand turn as Cunarder 1336, possibly en route for Coplawhill Works, turns from St. Vincent Street into Renfield Street and passes the impressive Bank of Scotland building. Heading east up St. Vincent Street is 1947 built Roberts bodied Albion Venturer B7 EGA 8.

201. The west side of Glasgow's famous George Square, viewed from Queen Street, with an unidentified hex dash Standard tram turning into St. Vincent Place. The North British Hotel has been replaced by the Copthorne.

202. James Watt, engineer and inventor, looks pre-occupied as Standard car 53 leads a Coronation car round the same corner, with a fine Morris Commercial Post Office van taking the other one.

203. Standard car 154 follows an elderly pre-war motor car round the corner past the magnificent Queen Street station arch, off George Square.

204. The atmosphere of Glasgow's City Centre is conveyed wonderfully here in this photograph, taken from an upper floor window in Union Street showing round dash Standard car 767.

205.   Back tracking along St. Vincent Place, we see Cunarder 1385 crossing over at the St. Vincent Street "City Centre" terminus of service 21, with Renfield Street behind. This may have been taken from a tour car, as this was the starting point for most city tram enthusiast tours.

206.   An evening scene showing Coronation car 1163 with its trafficator indicating a right hand turn from St. Vincent Street into Hope Street.

207. Heading all the way up Hope Street now, we see Coronation 1253 in an evening view, about to cross over Sauchiehall Street. The dome of the Theatre Royal, headquarters of Scottish Television, is in the distance.

208. This area, where Coronation 1155 turns from Hope Street into Cowcaddens, has seen dramatic changes to make way for motorways.

209. Another murky scene in Maitland Street where Coronation Mark 1 car 1153 waits to leave on a short journey to Gairbraid Avenue.

210. Along New City Road to St. George's Cross now, where round dash Standard car 620, looking bare without advertisements, clatters relentlessly over the St. George's Road track on a short working on service 29. The Empress Theatre, taken over by that much loved performer Jimmy Logan, is in the background.

211. Pausing a moment at this intersection, we see Standard hex dash car 48 in the opposite direction on the "29", with a view up Maryhill Road behind. This is now a quiet backwater – it's difficult to believe it was once a busy junction.

212. Coronation car 1284 pauses alongside the Olde Tramcar Vaults, a landmark in Maryhill Road famous for its "Room and Kitchen Car" model mounted above the window. The pub is demolished but the model is in the Peoples' Palace Museum on Glasgow Green.

213. Standard car 488 is seen again on the last day of service 18, June 3rd 1961, on the long bend in Maryhill Road where it meets Garscube Road at Queens Cross. A fellow tram enthusiast is taking photographs like Dougie from the rear compartment on the top deck.

214. The Standard car waiting in Gairbraid Avenue looks like 303, with a single decker Daimler bus, both dwarfed by the grim row of four storey tenements.

215. Rain clouds darken the scene as Coronation 1217 is flanked by a lovely red MG Magnette in Maryhill Road at Gairbraid Avenue on 20th October 1961. Service 29, which had a tight schedule, was replaced by motorbuses two days later.

216. Taken a year before, Coronation car 1393 with ex-Liverpool Green Goddess bogies is about to pass under the aqueduct carrying the Forth & Clyde Canal over Maryhill Road, on which our intrepid photographer is stationed. An elderly ornate lamp standard has survived, while the row of colourful advertisements brightens the rather drab scene.

217. This view is not one of Dougie's own but is part of his collection and is included as it shows a late red route band survivor at the Caldercuilt Road Maryhill terminus stub, also a car on service 40 outnumbered by the three on the "13". Maryhill terminus was moved from this cramped location to a new crossover on the wide expanse of Maryhill Road at Maryhill Park, to accommodate the "Green Goddesses".

218. Out at Killermont now, Standard car 43 heads for Milngavie, the most northerly outpost of the Glasgow tram system. On this wide stretch of road the police would occasionally flag down motormen doing speeds of up to 55 mph in Coronation and Green Goddess trams. The "offenders" would sheepishly reply, "but officer, the car disnae huv a speedometer".

219. A little further on, at Kessington, Standard car 75 passes the GCT sub-station at Bearsden, built in a style befitting its residential surroundings.

220. Taken on a lovely sunny day, Standard car 229 passes Lower Kilmardinny Farm showing the little used destination "Zoo".

221. Car 2 is also returning to town on the same stretch of road. Near here lay the rusting remnants of the Bennie Rail Plane, a monorail built in the 1920's by George Bennie, ahead of its time.

222. We have returned to Maryhill and see Coronation 1220 pulling out from under the aqueduct bridge in Bilsland Drive.

223. Coronation car 1223 grinds its way from the other side of the aqueduct up Bilsland Drive towards Ruchill.

224. Dougie is "up" to his tricks again here, with a view of Coronation 1251 about to pass under the railway bridge over Bilsland Drive nearer Possilpark.

225. Standard car 296 passes the Saracen Iron Works in Hawthorn Street, while a car on service 22 is returning to Possilpark Depot.

226. Further on now, a very smartly turned out car 86 approaches the bridge carrying the main Glasgow-Edinburgh railway line over Hawthorn Street not far from Springburn terminus.

227. Back to where Balmore Road crosses Hawthorn Street, for a short trip to Lambhill. Standard car 108 is seen at the Vogue Cinema.

228. Summer clothes are in evidence in these scenes as Standard car 457 passes between Possil and Possilpark stations in Balmore Road. Service 31 also served Lambhill but all of the four scenes here show cars on the "22". It was withdrawn first, in November 1958, the "31" lasting till November 1959.

229. A fine clear shot of Standard car 129 on the crest of the hill in Balmore Road, one or two stops from Lambhill terminus, passing tenement housing which went up in various parts of Glasgow such as Haghill and Blackhill in the early 1930's.

230. This is the Lambhill terminus in Strachur Street, a backwater with a mixture of olde world and new housing. I've been generous with this area as I have not seen many photographs of it. Beyond lies the newly developing Cadder housing scheme, to which tram 22 replacement bus service 54 was extended.

231. Before heading back into town for one last look there, we catch a glimpse of Keppochill Road not far from Saracen Street. The conductress and driver of Coronation 1146 are having a chat as the car passes Coldstream Place. Behind lies a row of grim looking tenements which the sunshine barely reaches. Not far from this spot is Pinkston Power Station, which generated the current for the tramway system.

232. Another view from an aqueduct, this time over Possil Road, with Coronation 1268 climbing up the slope towards Mosshouse.

233. Back to Charing Cross now, where the Grand Hotel buildings dwarf the Standard car making the sharp right hand turn from Sauchiehall Street into Woodlands Road – a view which is firmly in the past.

234. A wonderful scene which captures nicely the atmosphere of Sauchiehall Street, Glasgow's most famous thoroughfare. Tramcars, taxis, "classic" cars, shoppers, the Locarno, Malcolm Campbell's fruiterers' lorry, all part of the bustling city scene typical of the "Twilight Years".

235. A quieter scene in Parliamentary Road at Dundas Street Bus station, used by Alexander's and David Lawson's buses, with Coronation 1203 about to drop a passenger. I have a memento from the interior of this car, a small piece of wood showing its fleet number.

236. Car 183 passes a Gizzi's café at the Townhead end of "Parly" Road, at its junction with Monkland Street.

237. The old lady will hold up the Alexander's Leyland bus as she makes her unhurried way to the pavement at the east end of Parliamentary Road. Car 621 is on the Springburn circular 33 service. The dog relieving himself on the pavement looks as though he fancies a trip on the Cunarder to Millerston to escape from his run-down surroundings.

238. On our way home along Springburn Road, we pause at Charles Street to see hex dash Standard car 674 mounting the crest of the hill on its way into town.

239. Standard car 413 is seen just a few yards to the north, where the tracks were set to the right of the road. Another ornate elderly lamp standard survives from the pre First World War "dawn" of the Glasgow electric trams.

240. Dougie has gained access to the railway bridge to take this view of Coronation car 1223 ascending the long slope past St. Rollox Works. This bridge was the reason single deck cars were proposed at first in 1898, but the road was lowered in time for the opening to accommodate double deck cars.

241. A view which epitomises the industrial nature of this area, Douglas McMillan's heartland – the lone "Swan Vestas" advert adds only a little colour. Standard car 64 will reverse at the Elmvale Street Springburn terminus.

242. It has now done so and is captured on Dougie's camera again as it passes the brick building at the entrance to St. Rollox Railway Engineering Works, where he worked himself for much of his life.

243. On the home stretch, a Standard hex dash car with a fleet number in the forties, passes Petershill Road and will shortly round the curve into the "S" bend in the approach to Springburn. An elderly Daimler bus passes in the opposite direction showing "Private".

244. Well, we are back at Keppochill Road where we started and where it all began 100 years ago when electric trams ventured rather clumsily onto the streets of Glasgow. Standard car 109 passes two surgeries as it prepares to turn into Springburn Road.

245. 1179 was the last tram from Elmvale Street, Springburn terminus on 6th September 1958, when this photograph was probably taken of it, about to leave for Partick depot. It seems a fitting view with which to end this tour of Glasgow in the "twilight years", but there follows an epilogue which includes some views taken by Douglas which do not fit into any geographical order.

246. You feel you want to sit down on one of the moquette seats and soak up the atmosphere in this wonderful interior view of Standard car 404.

247. A top deck interior Standard car view now, taken in Argyle Street outside one of Britain's best known institutions, Marks & Spencer's, looking west, with the "Hielanman's Umbrella" in the distance. Like most youngsters, I would make for the front compartment where, with the door closed, you were in a world of your own – till the conductor came to take your fare.

248. A lower deck interior view of Coronation 1269 showing the "Alhambrinal" ceiling and lighting pattern. This car was originally selected for preservation by the STMS as it had its original lower deck light fittings, but it was found to be unsuitable and its bogies were placed under the body of car 1282, with the light fittings transferred too. That car runs today at the National Tramway Museum.

249. There is a fire tender in attendance as a Cunarder tram receives some attention possibly after an accident. Can anyone help with the location?

250. A review of the Twilight Years of Glasgow trams would not be complete without a brief look at the trolleybuses which replaced them. Here TB21, one of the original batch of BUT trolleybuses, appears to be approaching Riddrie terminus of service 101.

251. TB17, a Sunbeam trolleybus, crosses the junction of Cathcart Road with Crown Street at what is known as Gushetfaulds. Contrast the squat appearance of this vehicle with the previous one.

252. TB89, a later BUT trolleybus, turns from London Road into Bridgeton Cross on service 106. The trolleybuses themselves disappeared only five years after the trams.

253. With tongue in cheek I include this view of Edinburgh tram no. 35, as it is the only Edinburgh tram (as far as I know) to run in Glasgow, at the Garden Festival in 1988. It is seen here in the former Edinburgh Museum of Transport at Shrubhill, probably shortly after it opened in 1963.

254. I, Adam Gordon, am an interloper here to write my only caption. I remember visiting Wilmots temporary scrapyard at Partick, which this slide, taken by Colin Shewring, depicts. I also remember the man in charge pointing out the remains of no 1005, the Blue Devil, so even to the scrap man it had a significance & fame!

255. We are at the National Tramway Museum, Crich, in Derbyshire, where we see Standard car 812, alongside Sheffield car 46, in the early days of operation.

256. Glasgow 1068 is seen in its restored form as Paisley and District 68 at Crich. Hopefully this and other Glasgow trams here, at Summerlee and 1245 currently stored at Blackpool, will continue to run and give pleasure to a new generation of admirers of the tram-car, as well as a reminder of the Twilight Years of the Glasgow trams.

Thank
you   for
p u r c h a s i n g
this book, for in so
doing you are helping
to preserve car 1245, one of
Glasgow's "Coronation" tramcars, which were once described as
"the   finest   short-stage-vehicles   in
Europe". If anyone would like to sponsor
restoration work in return for publicity and
advertising space on car 1245, with the
possibility of it running during
millennium celebrations, or has
any other suggestions about
commercial   sponsor-
ship, Adam Gordon
will   be   very
pleased to
h e a r.

ADAM GORDON

Publisher and dealer in transport literature & ephemera

If you have enjoyed reading this book you may be interested in some of the following titles, many of them being reprints; * = hardback; obtainable from bookshops or direct from the publisher (address below); add 10% for postage and packing up to £5 maximum. No post and packing charge for orders of £50 or over.

Tramways of Reading.* H. Jordan, 2nd edition, 96pp, £12

Kidderminster and Stourport Electric Tramway Co Rules and Regulations, 1899, 58pp, £7

My Life in Many States and in Foreign Lands, G.F. Train, autobiography of street railway pioneer, who claimed that Jules Verne based "Around the world in 80 days" upon Train's own voyage; over 350pp, £12

Tramways and Electric Railways in the Nineteenth Century* (Electric Railway Number of Cassier's Magazine, 1899), cloth, over 250pp, £23

Tramways – their construction and working*, D.K. Clark, 2nd edn of 1894, over 750pp, 12 plates and over 400 line drawings, cloth, £32

Edinburgh Corporation Transport Department, timetable of electric tramways and motor buses June 1930, c.2 ¾" by 4 ¾" , 72pp, £6

London County Council Tramways guide to reopening of Kingsway Subway, 1931, coloured cover and map, 32pp £6

The Cable system of Tramway Traction 1896 – contemporary look at cable systems at home and abroad, 56pp, 6 photo pics and 2 line drawings, £10

The Feltham Car of the Metropolitan Electric and London United Tramways 1931, 18pp £5

The Overhaul of tramcars, London Transport, 26pp, 1935, £6

Tramway Review*, volumes 1 and 2, issues 1-16, 1950-1954, cloth h/b, includes articles on tramways in East Ham, Nottingham, Luton, Huddersfield, Barking, Sheffield, Oldham, Chester, Ilford, Wallasey, Leyton, Darlington, Cork, Lytham, Walthamstow, Isle of Man and Ireland, £23

Clippie, Z.Katin, a few months in the life of a tram and bus conductress in the war in Sheffield, 124pp £7

London Transport Bus routes, Central Area No 2 1943, folds out into c.11" by 17" – limited edition of 250 £5

Edinburgh Street Tramways Company Rules and Regulations for the servants, 1883, 56pp, limited edition of 250 £8

London County Council Tramways Motorman's Handbook, as from 1928, 32pp limited edition of 250 £6

The Training of Drivers and Conductors of Buses, Trams and Trolleybuses, London Transport, 1936, 20pp (250) £6

Double Century* by Stan Basnett and Keith Pearson. It comprises updated histories of the Upper Douglas Cable Tramway, and the Douglas Head Marine Drive Tramway. It also includes an appendix on the Cliff Lifts. Ch.4 consists of 'guided walks' along the routes today by Stan Basnett. It has 144 pages, including 8 in colour, and numerous illustrations; red buckram with gold lettering. £15.

My fifty years in transport – A.G. Grundy, 54pp, 26 illus, covers tramways of North Staffordshire, Blackburn, Potteries, Wrexham, and Stalybridge, Hyde, Mossley and Dukinfield. £10

Modern Tramway*, volumes 1 and 2, 1938 and 1939, reprinted and bound together in green cloth, sewn, gold lettering with original Light Rail Transit League logo on front, £38

How to go tram and tramway modelling – David Voice. Second edition of the title first published 16 years ago, now completely rewritten; coloured covers, 168 pages, 150 black & white photographs, 34 diagrams, and an illustrated glossary. £15.

Source book of literature relating to Scottish tramways – D. Croft & A. Gordon. Includes historical introduction and chronology, books, periodicals and major articles on specific tramway systems, legislation and accident reports, tramway museums and preservation, & rapid transit proposals. 48pp, £5.

All the above published by Adam Gordon, Priory Cottage, Chetwode, Nr. Buckingham, Bucks, MK18 4LB Tel: 01280 848650. [Trade terms, above prices less 35%, or more for multiple copies.]

Do you have anything of transport interest to sell? e.g. books, magazines, photographs, postcards, tickets, timetables, and ephemera – also hardware like ticket machines, racks and punches, enamelled signs, etc. Just ring or write to Adam Gordon above!